Perfect **PARTY** food

GW00721650

*A snack in the hand is worth eight on the plate, at least when you are at
a stand-up celebration, trying desperately to carry on a conversation
while juggling plate, glass, knife and fork.
This is the moment when finger food comes into its own. The recipes in this
collection have been chosen for eye appeal, ease of preparation and simplicity of
serving. Many of them can be made hours – or even days – ahead, and recipes
can be doubled or trebled where necessary to cater for large numbers.
Finger food might have been invented for picnics: adults can pick at the tempting
selection while younger members of the party nick nibbles in passing!
When packing food for portable feasts, prepare it as close as possible to the time of
departure, use sturdy (preferably insulated) containers, and avoid leaving
food in the sun or in cars for any length of time.
Remember to pack plenty of paper towels, wipes or wet flannels and
binbags for disposal of rubbish.
Pâtés, dips, quiches, sweet and savoury miniature pastries, finger
salads, sandwiches, brochettes and kebabs: they are all here, so whatever
the occasion, from casual picnic to sophisticated cocktail party, you can be
sure that good things come in small servings!*

CONTENTS

Pâtés and Dips

Some of the simplest snacks are also the most satisfying. Pâtés and dips take only minutes to make, but are certain to prove popular when served with crisp fresh vegetables, bread sticks or crisps.

Herb Liver Pâté

185g (6oz) butter

1 onion, chopped

2 cloves garlic, crushed

2 tspn fresh rosemary leaves

2 tblspn fresh thyme leaves

750g (1¹/₂lb) chicken livers, trimmed and roughly chopped

crackers for serving

sliced stuffed green olives for garnish

1 Melt 60g (2oz) butter in a frying pan. Add onion, garlic, rosemary and thyme and fry over low heat, until onion is soft. Set remaining butter aside to soften.

2 Add chicken livers to pan and fry, stirring occasionally, until just cooked through. Cool.

3 Purée mixture. Add softened butter; blend until smooth. Spoon pâté into a piping bag fitted with a large star nozzle; pipe onto crackers. Garnish with olive slices.

Makes about 30

Quick Chicken Liver Pâté

45g (1¹/₂oz) butter

2 tblspn chopped onion

250g (8oz) chicken livers, trimmed and roughly chopped

60ml (2fl oz) brandy, warmed

pinch tarragon

185ml (6fl oz) double cream, whipped

salt and freshly ground black pepper

1 Melt half the butter in a frying pan. Add onion and fry until soft. Remove onion from pan and set aside.

2 Melt remaining butter in pan and fry chicken livers until just cooked through. Add brandy and ignite.

3 Purée chicken livers with pan juices, reserved onion and tarragon in a blender or food processor. Stir in whipped cream, with salt and pepper to taste. Spoon into a serving dish, cover and chill until ready to serve.

Makes about 600ml (1pt)

Lazy Chicken Pâté

500g (1lb) cooked chicken, minced

1 small onion, finely chopped

2 hard-boiled eggs, mashed

60g (2oz) ground almonds

2 tblspn brandy

about 5 tblspn mayonnaise

salt and freshly ground black pepper

Tabasco sauce

pitted black olives, halved, for garnish

1 Combine chicken, onion, eggs, almonds and brandy in a bowl; mix well. Add enough mayonnaise to make a smooth paste. Season with salt, pepper and Tabasco.

2 Transfer pâté to a serving dish. Garnish with olive halves, cover and chill until ready to serve.

Makes about 750ml (1¹/₄pt)

Herb Liver Pâté

Mushrooms filled with Pâté and Bacon

185g (6oz) butter

750g (1½lb) chicken livers, trimmed and roughly chopped

185ml (6fl oz) port

salt and freshly ground black pepper

24 large cup mushrooms, stems removed

250g (8oz) rindless streaky bacon, chopped

1 Preheat oven to 180°C (350°F/ Gas 4). Melt butter in a frying pan, add livers and fry, stirring, for 2 minutes. Pour in port. Season with salt and pepper. Simmer until liver is just cooked.

2 Purée the mixture. Arrange mushrooms, cups uppermost, on a baking sheet. Fill with pâté mixture and top with bacon. Bake for 15 minutes or until bacon is cooked through.

Serves 24

Aubergine Dip

2 x 500g (1lb) aubergines, halved lengthwise

2 cloves garlic, roughly chopped

1 onion, chopped

125ml (4fl oz) white wine vinegar

2 tblspn sugar

1 tblspn soy sauce

1 tblspn Worcestershire sauce

freshly ground black pepper

1 Preheat oven to 200°C (400°F/ Gas 6). Prick skin of aubergines all over with a fork; place them cut side down on a baking sheet. Bake for 30 minutes or until aubergines are cooked and skin comes off easily. When cool enough to handle, peel aubergines and chop them roughly.

2 Purée aubergine with remaining ingredients. Spoon into a bowl, cover and chill for at least 1 hour before serving.

Makes about 500ml (16fl oz)

Curry Dip

2 hard-boiled eggs

1 tblspn mild curry powder

1 clove garlic, crushed

250ml (8fl oz) mayonnaise

1 tblspn lemon juice

2 tblspn finely chopped fresh parsley

salt

freshly ground black pepper

Tabasco sauce

1 Mash hard-boiled eggs with curry powder and garlic in a medium bowl.

2 Stir in the mayonnaise, lemon juice and parsley. Mix well.

3 Add salt, pepper and Tabasco to taste, transfer to a serving dish, cover and chill. Serve within 4 hours.

Makes about 300ml (10fl oz)

Mushrooms filled with Pâté and Bacon

Salmon Spread

250ml (8fl oz) chicken stock
2 medium salmon steaks
100g (3½oz) smoked salmon, chopped
200g (6½oz) butter, softened
1 tblspn lemon juice
2 tblspn red lumpfish roe

1 Bring stock to boil in a saucepan over moderate heat. Reduce to simmering and add salmon. Poach, covered, for 5 minutes or until cooked. Remove salmon and allow to cool.

2 Flake salmon, discarding skin and bones. Set aside.

3 Process smoked salmon, butter and lemon juice in a blender or food processor until smooth.

4 Transfer to a serving dish. Carefully stir in reserved salmon, then stir in lumpfish roe. Stir. Serve at room temperature.

Makes about 750g (1¼lb)

Salmon Spread

Tuna Pâté

200g (6½oz) drained canned tuna
125g (4oz) butter, softened, see Kitchen Tip
60ml (2fl oz) double cream or crème fraîche
½ tspn dry mustard
pinch cayenne
1 tblspn lemon juice
2 tblspn brandy
salt and freshly ground black pepper

1 Combine tuna, butter, cream, mustard, cayenne, lemon juice and brandy in a blender or food processor; process until smooth. Stir in salt and pepper to taste.

2 Transfer to a serving dish. Cover and refrigerate for at least 24 hours before serving.

Makes about 350ml (12fl oz)

Kitchen Tip
Make sure the butter is very soft, or the pâté will be crumbly when set.

Creamy Sardine Dip

250g (8oz) cream cheese
60ml (2fl oz) lemon juice
2 x 120g (4oz) cans sardines in oil
3 tblspn snipped chives
3 tblspn chopped fresh parsley
single cream, see method

1 Purée cream cheese and lemon juice in a blender or food processor until creamy and soft. Add sardines with oil; process again.

2 Add chives and parsley, process to mix, then beat in enough cream to give the dip the desired consistency.

3 Spoon into a bowl, cover and refrigerate.

Makes about 500ml (16fl oz)

Summer Dip

2 hard-boiled eggs, chopped
1 clove garlic, crushed
250ml (8fl oz) mayonnaise
2 tblspn lemon juice
2 tblspn chopped pitted green olives
2 tblspn chopped gherkins
2 tblspn chopped capers

1 Mash the hard-boiled eggs with the garlic in a medium bowl.

2 Stir in the mayonnaise, lemon juice, olives, gherkins and capers; mix well. Transfer to a serving dish, cover and chill until ready to serve.

Makes about 300ml (10fl oz)

Trout and Prawn Pâté

90g (3oz) butter

4 spring onions, finely chopped

2 cloves garlic, crushed

500g (1lb) trout fillets, skinned and roughly chopped

2 tblspn brandy

500g (1lb) peeled cooked prawns, deveined

125ml (4fl oz) single cream

1 tblspn lemon juice

2 tblspn chopped dill

2 tspn chilli sauce, optional

salt and freshly ground black pepper

1 Melt butter in a saucepan. Add spring onions and garlic and cook for 1 minute.

2 Remove bones from trout. Add trout to pan. Stir over gentle heat until cooked. Add brandy and cook for 1 minute, then stir in prawns, cream, lemon juice, dill and chilli sauce.

3 Transfer to a blender or food processor; purée until smooth. Add salt and pepper to taste. Spoon into a serving dish, cover and refrigerate until firm.

Makes about 1kg (2lb)

Smoked Fish Pâté

155g (5oz) smoked mackerel, skinned and boned

155g (5oz) smoked trout, skinned and boned

155g (5oz) smoked salmon, skinned and boned

90g (3oz) butter, softened

100ml (3 1/2fl oz) natural low fat yogurt

3 tblspn snipped chives

3 tblspn lemon juice

1/2 tspn freshly ground black pepper

Purée all ingredients in a blender or food processor; until smooth. Transfer to a serving dish, cover and refrigerate until ready to serve.

Makes about 560g (1lb 2oz)

Chilli Cheese Dip

90g (3oz) green chillies, seeded and chopped

1 red chilli, seeded and chopped

90g (3oz) mature Cheddar cheese, chopped

dash Worcestershire sauce

2 spring onions, chopped

salt

freshly ground black pepper

milk or single cream, optional

1 Combine all ingredients except milk in a blender or food processor. Process until light and fluffy. If mixture is too thick, thin with a little milk or cream.

2 Transfer to a serving dish, cover and refrigerate for about 1 hour before serving.

Makes about 500ml (16fl oz)

Roquefort Avocado Dip

2 ripe avocados, halved, stoned and peeled

60g (2oz) Roquefort cheese, crumbled

2 tblspn soured cream

1 tblspn lemon juice

olive oil, see method

freshly ground black pepper

1 Mash the avocados in a bowl. Add the cheese and soured cream and mix well.

2 Stir in the lemon juice and add enough oil to give a smooth paste. Season with black pepper.

3 Transfer to a serving dish, cover closely and refrigerate until ready to serve.

Makes about 350ml (12fl oz)

Dill Dip

1 tspn Dijon mustard

1 tspn white wine vinegar

2 tblspn olive oil

150ml (5fl oz) soured cream

2 tblspn finely chopped fresh dill

1 tlspn finely chopped fresh parsley

2 cloves garlic, crushed

salt

freshly ground black pepper

1 Combine the mustard and vinegar in a small bowl. Whisk well, gradually adding the olive oil until the mixture is well combined.

2 Add the soured cream, dill, parsley and garlic, with salt and pepper to taste. Mix well. Transfer to a serving dish and serve with crisp fresh vegetable dippers.

Makes about 185ml (6fl oz)

Stilton and Ricotta Dip

125g (4oz) Stilton cheese, crumbled

250g (8oz) ricotta or full-fat cream cheese

150ml (5fl oz) whipping cream

1/2 red pepper, finely chopped

salt, optional

freshly ground black pepper

1 Mash the Stilton cheese in a bowl until smooth. Add the ricotta gradually, mixing the cheeses together thoroughly.

2 In a second bowl, whip the cream until soft peaks form. Fold into the cheese mixture with the chopped red pepper. Add salt, if required, and pepper to taste. Transfer to a serving dish, cover and refrigerate for I hour before serving.

Makes about 600ml (1pt)

Smoked Fish Pâté

7

PERFECT FOR PICNICS

Cut-and-come-again flans, quiches and pizzas make ideal picnic fare. To complete the spread for an alfresco feast, this chapter includes sandwiches, finger salads, filo pastries and a tempting terrine.

Ricotta and Olive Flan

Pastry

155g (5oz) cold butter, cubed

250g (8oz) plain flour

3-4 tblspn iced water

Filling

200g (6½oz) ricotta cheese

90g (3oz) grated Parmesan cheese

30g (1oz) fresh white breadcrumbs

3 eggs, lightly beaten

125ml (4fl oz) single cream

90g (3oz) stuffed green olives, sliced

1 Rub the butter into the flour in a medium bowl until the mixture resembles fine breadcrumbs. Add enough iced water to form a dough. Wrap in greaseproof paper and chill for 30 minutes.

2 Preheat oven to 190°C (375°F/ Gas 5). On a lightly floured surface, roll out pastry to fit a 23cm (9in) flan tin. Prick the base with a fork and bake for 10 minutes.

3 Combine the ricotta, Parmesan, breadcrumbs, eggs and cream in a large bowl; mix well. Stir in the sliced olives, reserving some to decorate the top of the flan.

4 Pour the filling into the pie shell. Decorate with the reserved olive slices. Bake for 35 minutes. Transport to the picnic in the tin.

Serves 6

Pea and Sweetcorn Flan

1 x 215g (7oz) packet frozen shortcrust pastry, thawed

30g (1oz) butter

2 tblspn plain flour

300ml (10fl oz) milk

1 x 340g (11oz) can whole kernel sweetcorn, drained

125g (4oz) peas, cooked

4 spring onions, chopped

freshly ground black pepper

2 eggs, lightly beaten

125g (4oz) mature Cheddar cheese, grated

1 Preheat oven to 190°C (375°F/ Gas 5). Roll out the pastry on a lightly floured surface to fit a 23cm (9in) flan tin. Prick the base with a fork and bake for 10 minutes.

2 Melt the butter in a saucepan over moderate heat. Add the flour and cook, stirring, for 1 minute. Gradually add the milk, stirring until the mixture boils and thickens. Stir in the corn, peas and spring onions, with pepper to taste.

3 Remove the pan from the heat, cool slightly, then stir in the eggs.

4 Pour the mixture into the pastry shell, sprinkle with cheese and bake for 30 minutes or until golden brown. Transport to the picnic in the tin.

Serves 6

Pea and Sweetcorn Flan

Blue Cheese and Onion Quiche

Chèvre and Nut Quiche

Pastry

250g (8oz) plain flour

salt

185g (6oz) very cold butter, cubed

1 ½ tblspn iced water

Filling

5 lettuce leaves, finely shredded

3 spring onions, finely chopped

2 tblspn chopped fresh coriander

1 clove garlic, crushed

185g (6oz) Chèvre (goats' cheese) crumbled

3 large eggs

300ml (10fl oz) single cream

salt

freshly ground black pepper

2 tblspn walnut oil

2 tblspn grated Parmesan cheese

30g (1oz) walnuts, chopped

1 Make pastry. Combine flour and salt in a bowl and rub in butter until mixture resembles fine breadcrumbs. Add enough iced water to make a dough. Shape dough to a flattish round, wrap and refrigerate for 1 hour.

2 Preheat oven to 190°C (375°F/ Gas 5). On a lightly floured surface, roll out dough to fit a 23cm (9in) flan tin. Prick base with a fork and bake for 10 minutes.

3 Arrange lettuce and spring onions in pastry shell. Sprinkle with coriander, garlic and Chèvre.

4 In a bowl, beat eggs with cream. Season and pour into pastry shell. Bake for 25 minutes.

5 Remove quiche from oven, brush with walnut oil and sprinkle with Parmesan cheese and walnuts. Cook for 10 minutes more or until set.

Serves 6

Blue Cheese and Onion Quiche

1 x 215g (7oz) packet frozen shortcrust pastry, thawed

30g (1oz) butter

3 onions, thinly sliced

2 cloves garlic, crushed

3 eggs

60g (2oz) blue cheese, crumbled

250ml (8fl oz) milk

185ml (6fl oz) soured cream

freshly ground black pepper

2 tspn caraway seeds

1 Preheat oven to 190°C (375°F/ Gas 5). Roll out pastry on a lightly floured surface to fit a 23cm (9in) flan tin. Prick base with a fork and bake for 10 minutes.

2 Melt butter in a frying pan over gentle heat. Add onions and garlic and fry, stirring frequently, for 10 minutes or until onions are soft and golden brown. Transfer onions and garlic to pastry shell.

3 In a bowl, beat eggs lightly. Stir in cheese, milk and soured cream, with pepper to taste. Add caraway seeds. Pour mixture over onions.

4 Bake for 30 minutes or until crust of the quiche is golden and filling is lightly firm.

Serves 6

Onion and Soured Cream Quiche

1 x 215g (7oz) packet frozen shortcrust pastry, thawed

75g (2¹/₂oz) butter

6 large onions, sliced

1 Granny Smith apple, sliced

salt and freshly ground black pepper

grated nutmeg

¹/₂ tspn caraway seeds

300ml (10fl oz) soured cream

3 eggs, beaten

1 Preheat oven to 190°C (375°F/ Gas 5). Roll out the pastry on a lightly floured surface to fit a 23cm (9in) flan tin. Prick the base with a fork and bake for 10 minutes.

2 Melt 60g (2oz) of butter in a frying pan. Cook onions and apple over low heat for 30 minutes, turning occasionally. Drain. Season with salt, pepper and nutmeg. Stir in caraway seeds. Spread mixture in pastry shell.

3 Mix soured cream and eggs together; pour into pastry shell and dot with remaining butter. Bake for 30-35 minutes until set.

Serves 6

Brie and Bacon Quiche

1 x 215g (7oz) packet frozen shortcrust pastry, thawed

185g (6oz) rindless streaky bacon, chopped

1 onion, chopped

2 cloves garlic, crushed

2 tblspn chopped fresh parsley

4 eggs, lightly beaten

300ml (10fl oz) double cream

¹/₄ tspn freshly ground black pepper

2 drained canned pimientos, chopped

200g (6¹/₂oz) Brie cheese, thinly sliced

¹/₄ tspn grated nutmeg

1 Preheat oven to 190°C (375°F/ Gas 5). Roll out pastry on a lightly floured surface to fit a 23cm (9in) flan tin. Prick base with a fork and bake for 10 minutes.

2 Heat bacon in a frying pan until fat runs, then raise heat, add onion and fry over moderate heat for 3 minutes. Stir in garlic and parsley and cook for 2 minutes more.

3 Meanwhile, combine eggs, cream and pepper in a large jug. Mix well.

4 Using a slotted spoon, transfer bacon and onion mixture to pastry shell. Arrange chopped pimientos on top. Carefully pour egg mixture into pastry shell.

5 Arrange Brie slices on top of the filling, sprinkle with nutmeg and bake for about 40 minutes until set. Transport to picnic in tin.

Serves 6

Brie and Bacon Quiche

Vegetable Pizza

90g (3oz) plain flour

1/2 tspn sugar

1/2 tspn salt

1/2 x 7g (1/4oz) sachet easy blend dried yeast

1 tblspn olive oil

60ml (2fl oz) warm water

Topping

2 tblspn tomato purée

125g (4oz) cottage cheese

1 onion, sliced

1 red pepper, sliced

60g (2oz) button mushrooms, sliced

8-10 black olives

60g (2oz) grated Parmesan cheese

1 Combine the flour, sugar, salt and yeast in a large bowl. Stir in oil and warm water. Mix to a dough, then turn onto a lightly floured surface and knead for about 5 minutes until smooth and elastic.

2 Place the dough in an oiled bowl, cover with clingfilm and a tea towel. Stand in a warm place until doubled in bulk.

3 Preheat oven to 190°C (375°F/ Gas 5). Knead the dough for 2 minutes, roll it out and use to line a lightly oiled 28cm (11in) pizza pan.

4 Spread tomato purée evenly over dough. Cover with cottage cheese. Arrange onion rings, pepper slices and mushrooms on top and dot with olives. Sprinkle with cheese and bake for 20 minutes. Transport to picnic in pan.

Serves 6-8

Variations

A variety of vegetables may be used to top this pizza. Try sliced canned artichoke hearts, sliced canned celery hearts, sun-dried tomatoes, sliced canned pimientos, lightly cooked leeks or courgettes. Vary the cheeses – try grated Cheddar, sliced mozzarella or grated Red Leicester cheese.

Smoked Ham Pinwheels

1 small uncut white loaf

250g (8oz) cream cheese, softened

2 tblspn Dijon mustard

4 tblspn chopped fresh parsley

250g (8oz) smoked ham, sliced

1 Remove crusts from loaf. Slice it lengthwise into 5 slices. Flatten slices with a rolling pin.

2 Combine cream cheese, mustard and parsley in a bowl. Mix well. Spread on bread slices, cover with ham and roll up from one long side. Wrap in foil and place in freezer.

3 About 5 hours before serving remove ham rolls from freezer. When still partially frozen, slice each roll into 5 pinwheels.

Makes 25

Smoked Salmon Mini Quiches

1 x 215g (7oz) packet frozen puff pastry, thawed

125g (4oz) smoked salmon, chopped

250ml (8fl oz) double cream

3 eggs, lightly beaten

2 tspn grated lemon rind

pinch grated nutmeg

2 tspn chopped fresh dill

freshly ground black pepper

1 Preheat oven to 190°C (375°F/ Gas 5). Roll out pastry thinly on a lightly floured surface. Using a fluted 6cm (2 1/2in) cutter, cut out circles and press into shallow tartlet tins.

2 Divide smoked salmon between pastry cases. Combine cream, eggs, lemon rind, nutmeg and dill. Season with pepper. Fill pastry cases no more than two-thirds full. Bake for 10 minutes until puffed and golden.

Makes about 24

Smoked Salmon Mini Quiches

Crusty Parmesan Chicken Drumsticks

4 tblspn Dijon mustard

4 tblspn oil

4 tblspn finely chopped spring onions

1/4 tspn freshly ground black pepper

30g (1oz) grated Parmesan cheese

8 chicken drumsticks

60g (2oz) dried breadcrumbs

60g (2oz) butter, melted

1 Preheat oven to 180°C (350°F/ Gas 4). Mix the mustard, oil, spring onions, pepper and Parmesan in a medium bowl.

2 Using a pastry brush, coat each chicken drumstick in the mustard cheese mixture, then roll them in the breadcrumbs to coat completely.

3 Arrange the drumsticks on a baking sheet, drizzle with the melted butter and bake for 30 minutes or until cooked through, turning twice.

Serves 4

Meat Loaf in a Bread Crust

1 large round loaf of bread

2 tblspn oil

1 onion, finely chopped

1 clove garlic, crushed

500g (1lb) minced steak

250g (8oz) drained canned chopped tomatoes

1 tblspn tomato purée

2 tspn chopped fresh parsley

salt

freshly ground black pepper

1 Preheat oven to 180°C (350°F/ Gas 4). Invert loaf of bread and carefully cut a circle, about 13cm (5in) across, from centre of base. Set circle aside. Scoop out most of bread from inside of loaf; crumb in a food processor. Set aside 6 tablespoons of the breadcrumbs. Freeze the remainder for later use.

2 Heat oil in a saucepan and fry onion and garlic until softened. Using a slotted spoon, transfer onion and garlic to a bowl. Set aside.

3 Add minced steak to pan. Cook, stirring frequently, until browned. Drain off excess fat. Return onion and garlic to pan. Stir in chopped tomatoes, tomato purée and parsley, with salt and pepper to taste. Bring mixture to boil, then simmer for 30 minutes until thickened. Cool slightly; stir in reserved breadcrumbs.

4 Spoon filling into hollowed-out bread loaf; replace crust circle. Cover loaf with a large piece of foil, then carefully invert loaf and foil onto a baking sheet. Bring up foil to enclose loaf completely. Bake for 20 minutes. Wrap in a second layer of foil before transporting to the picnic. Cut in slices to serve.

Serves 6

Crusty Parmesan Chicken Drumsticks

Julienne Salad

Cold Roast Beef with Capers and Anchovies

The ingredients for this salad can be packed separately and assembled at the picnic.

10 slices cold roast beef

10 slices mozzarella cheese

8 anchovy fillets

2 tblspn drained capers

5 tblspn olive oil

1/2 tspn crushed black peppercorns

2 tblspn lemon juice

1 tblspn chopped fresh parsley

1 Arrange beef and cheese slices alternately on a large platter.

2 Add the anchovy fillets and capers. Mix the remaining ingredients together and pour them over the salad.

Serves 4-5

Marinated Prawns

2 tblspn oil

2 tblspn red wine vinegar

1 tblspn snipped chives

1 clove garlic, crushed

dash Tabasco sauce

salt and freshly ground black pepper

24 peeled cooked prawns, deveined

paprika

1 Combine oil, vinegar, chives, garlic and Tabasco sauce in a screwtop jar. Close tightly and shake until well mixed. Add salt and pepper to taste.

2 Place prawns in a bowl, pour over dressing, cover and marinate in refrigerator for 12 hours or overnight, stirring occasionally. Serve sprinkled with paprika.

Makes 24

Julienne Salad

If the dressing is omitted, these vegetable sticks (julienne) are ideal for serving with any of the dips in the previous chapter.

125g (4oz) carrots, cut in thin sticks

2 courgettes, cut in thin sticks

1 red pepper, cut in thin sticks

1 green pepper, cut in thin sticks

1 stick celery, cut in thin strips

4 spring onions, cut in short lengths

1 tblspn tarragon vinegar

2 tblspn walnut oil

1 clove garlic, crushed

Place vegetables in a salad bowl. Combine vinegar, oil and garlic in a screwtop jar, and shake until well mixed. Pour over salad and toss well. Cover and refrigerate for 3 hours before serving.

Serves 4

Spinach and Feta Filo Triangles

1 x 275g (9oz) packet filo pastry (12 sheets)

90g (3oz) butter, melted

Filling

1 onion, chopped

30ml (1fl oz) oil

250g (8oz) frozen spinach, thawed

125g (4oz) feta cheese

185g (6oz) cream cheese

2 eggs, beaten

3 tblspn fresh white breadcrumbs

1 Preheat oven to 190°C (375°F/ Gas 5). Fry onion in oil in a frying pan until soft. Add spinach, mix well and cook until moisture has evaporated, stirring occasionally.

2 Crumble feta into a bowl. Add cream cheese and eggs; mix well. Stir in breadcrumbs and spinach.

3 Without unfolding feta sheets, cut them with a pair of scissors into strips 5cm (2in) wide. Unroll one strip at a time, covering the remainder with a tea towel.

4 Brush pastry strip generously with melted butter. Place a heaped teaspoonful of filling on one end of strip so that the corner of strip can be folded diagonally over it to form a triangle. Continue folding strip over on itself, retaining triangular shape. Brush with butter and place on a baking sheet. Repeat, using remaining pastry strips and filling. Bake for 10-12 minutes or until golden.

Makes about 60

Variation

Fry the onion in the oil as above. In a bowl, combine 185g (6oz) fromage frais, 90g (3oz) grated Cheddar cheese and 1/2 tspn lemon juice. Mix well. Stir in the onion. Finely chop 5 drained canned artichoke hearts;add to the filling mixture, with salt and pepper to taste. Use as suggested above.

Tuna and Asparagus Filo Squares

60ml (2fl oz) olive oil

4 spring onions, chopped

3 eggs, beaten

125ml (4fl oz) single cream

1 tblspn flour

250g (8oz) cottage cheese

1 tblspn lemon juice

1 x 185g (6oz) can tuna in brine, drained and flaked

1 tblspn chopped fresh parsley

1 x 275g (9oz) packet filo pastry (12 sheets)

1 x 340g (11oz) can asparagus spears, drained

1 Heat 1 tablespoon of oil in a small pan and fry spring onions for 3 minutes over gentle heat. Set aside to cool, then tip into a bowl and add eggs, cream, flour, cottage cheese, lemon juice, tuna and parsley. Mix well.

2 Preheat oven to 180°C (350°F/ Gas 4). Line a lightly oiled 20cm (8in) square baking tin with one sheet of filo, allowing sides of filo to rise up sides of tin. Lightly brush with some of the remaining oil. Repeat with 5 more sheets.

3 Spoon filling into filo-lined tin. Top with drained asparagus. Cover with another sheet of filo, brushing it with oil. Repeat with 4 more filo sheets. Cover with final sheet of filo, tucking overlap down sides of tin. Brush top with oil.

4 Bake for 40 minutes or until filo is crisp and golden. Cut into squares to serve.

Makes 16

Kitchen Tip

Sprinkle the top layer of filo with a few drops of water before baking; this will prevent the pastry from curling up.

Spinach and Feta Filo Triangles

Country Terrine

For best results, allow the terrine to stand in the refrigerator for 2 days before serving.

1.5kg (3lb) coarse fatty minced pork and veal
30g (1oz) butter
1 small onion, finely chopped
1 clove garlic, crushed
250g (8oz) chicken livers, trimmed
2 tblspn soft white breadcrumbs
3 tblspn chopped fresh parsley
2 eggs, beaten
125ml (4fl oz) single cream
60ml (2fl oz) brandy
1 tspn salt
1 tspn freshly ground black pepper
1/2 tspn grated nutmeg
1/4 tspn ground allspice
500g (1lb) rindless streaky bacon rashers
125g (4oz) thickly sliced prosciutto, cut into strips
60g (2oz) shelled pistachio nuts

1 Preheat oven to 180°C (350°F/ Gas 4). Place minced meat in a large bowl. Melt butter in a frying pan, add onion and garlic and cook until onion is soft, stirring occasionally.

2 Add chicken livers to pan; sauté over moderate heat for 5 minutes or until livers spring back to the touch. Purée until smooth.

3 Add mixture to minced meat. Stir in breadcrumbs and parsley, then add eggs, cream, brandy, salt, pepper, nutmeg and allspice. Mix well.

4 Line a large loaf tin with bacon, letting excess hang over sides. Make a layer of half meat mixture, followed by prosciutto strips and pistachios in lengthwise rows. Top with remaining meat mixture.

5 Fold bacon strips over top. Cover tin securely with foil. Place in a roasting tin, add boiling water to come halfway up loaf tin and cook for 2 1/2 hours, topping up water if necessary.

6 Remove tin from oven; cool for 30 minutes. Place a heavy weight on top of terrine (a second tin filled with cans or a wrapped brick is ideal). Place in refrigerator. Remove the weight after 4 hours.

Serves 12

Smoked Trout and Asparagus Terrine

4 tblspn powdered gelatine
60ml (2fl oz) water
750ml (1 1/4pt) hot fish or chicken stock
1 1/2 tspn crushed black peppercorns
1 smoked trout, head, bones and skin removed, broken into small pieces
2 tblspn chopped fresh herbs
12 canned asparagus spears

1 Sprinkle the gelatine onto the measured water in a small bowl. When spongy, stir into the hot stock until completely dissolved. Add the crushed peppercorns. Set the stock aside to cool completely.

2 Lightly oil a 750ml (1 1/4pt) loaf tin. Pour in the stock to fill the tin to one third of its depth. Refrigerate for 1 hour or until set.

3 Arrange the trout pieces on top of the set aspic, sprinkle the herbs over the top and pour on enough stock to cover by 1cm (1/2in). Refrigerate for 1 hour or until set.

4 Lay the asparagus spears on top of the terrine and carefully add the remaining stock. Refrigerate for 1 hour or until set. When ready to serve, gently ease the terrine out onto a serving plate. Serve in slices.

Serves 6

Marinated Mushrooms

Prosciutto Wrapped Asparagus

12 fresh asparagus spears

4 slices prosciutto

1 Boil or steam the asparagus until tender. Drain, rinse under cold water and drain again.

2 Cut the prosciutto lengthwise into 3 long strips. Wrap a strip of prosciutto around each asparagus spear. Garnish with parsley and chilli flowers when serving, if liked.

Makes 12

Marinated Mushrooms

500g (1lb) small button mushrooms, trimmed

250ml (8fl oz) boiling water

2 tblspn lemon juice

5 tblspn olive oil

2 tblspn white wine vinegar

2 cloves garlic, crushed

2 tspn thyme leaves

1 tblspn chopped parsley

1 Put the button mushrooms in a heatproof bowl. Mix the boiling water and lemon juice, pour over the mushrooms and set aside for 5 minutes. Drain.

2 Combine the oil, vinegar, garlic, thyme and parsley in a screwtop jar. Close tightly, shake well, then pour the dressing over the mushrooms. Cover and refrigerate for at least 2 hours, preferably overnight.

Makes about 30

Prosciutto Wrapped Asparagus

Celebrate summer with a party on the patio or in the garden. Time spent on preparation will be amply rewarded when guests tuck in to mouthwatering morsels like Lamb and Coconut Satay, Continental Salad Sticks and Bacon Wrapped Prawns.

Prawn Boats

300ml (10fl oz) soured cream

1 tblspn drained capers, chopped

1 tblspn Dijon mustard

2 tblspn snipped chives

6 sticks celery, cut into 5cm (2in) lengths

375g (12oz) medium cooked prawns, deveined

1 tblspn caviar or red lumpfish roe

1 Combine the soured cream, capers and mustard in a bowl. Add half the chives and mix well.

2 Spoon the mixture into the celery sticks. Top each filled celery stick with a prawn and a dab of caviar or lumpfish roe. Garnish with the remaining snipped chives.

Makes about 24

Herb Filled Cherry Tomatoes

45g (1¹/₂oz) slivered almonds

500g (1lb) cherry tomatoes

125g (4oz) cream cheese

1 tblspn chopped fresh mint

1 tblspn chopped fresh parsley

1 tblspn snipped chives

1 Toast the almonds under the grill, watching them carefully to prevent scorching. Chop roughly.

2 Cut the top off each tomato. Scoop out the seeds; reserve 2 tablespoons of the pulp.

Herb Filled Cherry Tomatoes

3 In a bowl, beat the cream cheese until smooth. Stir in the almonds, mint, parsley, chives and reserved tomato pulp.

4 Spoon the filling into the tomatoes. Refrigerate for 1 hour or until firm. Serve on a tray, garnished with coriander, if liked.

Makes about 36

Devilled Eggs

12 eggs

2 tblspn mayonnaise

1 tblspn single cream

1 tspn dry mustard

1 tspn curry powder

Garnishes
Choose from: caviar, chopped spring onions, chives, shrimps, olives, radishes, gherkins, cherry tomatoes, toasted almonds, dill, watercress

1 Place eggs in a large saucepan with cold water to cover. Stir gently over heat until water boils (this keeps yolks centred). Reduce heat and simmer, without stirring, for 10 minutes, then drain. Run under cold water until eggs have cooled.

2 Shell eggs; cut them in half lengthwise. Taking care not to damage whites, spoon out yolks and combine with mayonnaise, cream, mustard and curry powder. Stir until smooth.

3 Spoon yolk mixture into a piping bag fitted with a star nozzle. Fill whites and garnish.

Makes 24

Lamb and Coconut Satay

500g (1lb) lean minced lamb

1 tblspn tomato purée

3 tblspn desiccated coconut

1 tspn ground cumin

2 tblspn chopped fresh coriander

1 tblspn chopped fresh parsley

3 tblspn freshly squeezed lime juice

1 Soak short wooden skewers in cold water for 1 hour. Preheat grill. Combine lamb, tomato purée, coconut, cumin, coriander, parsley and lime juice. Mix well. Roll tablespoons of mixture into balls. Thread 3 balls onto each skewer.

2 Grill satays for 3 minutes each side or until cooked.

Serves 4-6

Lamb and Coconut Satay

Chicken Teriyaki Skewers

4 chicken breast fillets

8 spring onions, cut into 1cm (1/2in) lengths

Mustard Dipping Sauce

125ml (4fl oz) mayonnaise

5 tblspn Dijon mustard

1 tspn Worcestershire sauce

1/2 tspn chilli sauce

Marinade

125ml (4fl oz) sherry

125ml (4fl oz) soy sauce

60ml (2fl oz) oil

45g (1 1/2oz) dark brown sugar

2 cloves garlic, crushed

freshly ground black pepper

1 Make dipping sauce by mixing all ingredients in a bowl. Cover; refrigerate for 3 hours.

2 Combine all marinade ingredients in a large shallow bowl. Mix well. Cut each chicken breast into 12 pieces. Add to marinade and stir to coat. Cover; marinate for 2 hours.

3 Soak 24 short wooden skewers in cold water for 1 hour. Preheat grill. Drain chicken. Reserve marinade. Thread 2 chicken pieces alternately with spring onion onto each skewer.

4 Grill, for 2-3 minutes on each side, basting with reserved marinade. Serve with the dipping sauce.

Makes 24

Curried Minced Beef Kebabs with Yogurt Tomato Sauce

500g (1lb) lean minced beef

50g (2oz) desiccated coconut

2 eggs, lightly beaten

1 tblspn tomato purée

2 tspn ground coriander

2 tspn ground cumin

60ml (2fl oz) coconut cream

2 tspn curry powder

4 cloves garlic, crushed

2 tomatoes, chopped into very small dice

1 tblspn chopped fresh coriander

185ml (6fl oz) low fat natural yogurt

1 Preheat grill. Combine minced beef, coconut, eggs, tomato purée, ground coriander and cumin, coconut cream and curry powder in a large bowl. Stir in half the garlic; mix well. Shape mixture into small sausages, thread onto short metal skewers and grill until cooked through, turning frequently.

2 Meanwhile, combine remaining garlic with tomatoes, fresh coriander and yogurt in a small bowl. Mix well; serve with kebabs.

Makes about 16

Red Pepper Pancakes with Spring Onions

1 red pepper, chopped

125g (4oz) ricotta cheese

2 egg whites

30g (1oz) flour

1/2 tspn crushed black peppercorns

1/2 onion, roughly chopped

8 spring onions, cut into big strips

1 In a blender or food processor, blend the red pepper with the ricotta, eggs, flour, pepper and onion for about 2 minutes.

2 Heat a nonstick frying pan over moderate heat. Drop tablespoonfuls of the batter into the pan, leaving plenty of room for spreading. As each pancake turns golden underneath, flip it over and cook until the other side browns.

3 Remove the pancakes from the heat, place a few strips of spring onion on each and roll up. Serve immediately.

Makes 12

Red Pepper Pancakes with Spring Onions

Pizza Muffins

These go down well with younger guests.

12 wholewheat muffins, cut in half

125g (4oz) butter, softened

2 tblspn tomato purée

4 carrots, grated

4 sticks celery, finely chopped

125g (4oz) sliced cooked ham, chopped

250g (8oz) mozzarella cheese, thinly sliced

1 Preheat grill. Butter each muffin half. Toast under grill until golden.

2 Spread each muffin thinly with tomato puree. Top with carrot, celery, ham and mozzarella. Place under hot grill until cheese melts. Serve at once.

Makes 24

Mini Lamb Burgers with Creamy Mustard Sauce

500g (1lb) lean minced lamb

3 tblspn fresh white breadcrumbs

1/4 tspn cayenne pepper

2 tblspn sweet fruit chutney

1 tblspn chopped fresh parsley

1 tblspn snipped chives

12 small bread rolls, halved

2 courgettes, shredded

1 carrot, shredded

4 tblspn chopped fresh parsley

60g (2oz) cream cheese, softened

Creamy Mustard Sauce

2 tblspn Dijon mustard

2 tblspn double cream

2 tspn lemon juice

1/4 tspn crushed black peppercorns

1 Make Creamy Mustard Sauce. Combine mustard, cream, lemon juice and peppercorns in a blender or food processor. Blend until smooth. Spoon into a small bowl and set aside.

2 Preheat grill. Combine lamb, breadcrumbs, cayenne, chutney, parsley and chives in a medium bowl. Mix thoroughly. Shape into 12 mini-burgers. Grill under moderate heat, turning frequently, until cooked through.

3 Toast cut sides of buns. Arrange bases of rolls on a serving platter. Place a burger on each base and top with courgette and carrot shreds. Add a sprinkling of parsley and a dollop of creamy mustard. Top with bun 'lids'. Serve with remaining mustard sauce.

Makes 12

Pork and Veal Terrine with Pimiento and Olives

2 tblspn olive oil

250g (8oz) button mushrooms, sliced

750g (1½lb) minced pork

1 x 400g (13oz) can pimientos, drained and finely chopped

30g (1oz) fresh white breadcrumbs

60g (2oz) pitted black olives, sliced

60g (2oz) sun-dried tomatoes in oil, drained and chopped

2 cloves garlic, crushed

2 tblspn chopped fresh basil

2 tspn red wine vinegar

¼ tspn grated nutmeg

1 egg, lightly beaten

salt

freshly ground black pepper

1 Preheat oven to 180°C (350°F/ Gas 4). Heat oil in a heavy-based frying pan, add mushrooms and fry for about 5 minutes, stirring frequently, until juices are released. Set aside.

2 Combine minced pork, pimientos, breadcrumbs, olives, sun-dried tomatoes, garlic, basil, vinegar, nutmeg and beaten egg in a large bowl. Using a slotted spoon, transfer mushrooms to bowl. Mix well, first with a spoon and then with clean hands. Season to taste with plenty of salt and pepper.

3 Line a 20 x 11cm (8 x 4½in) loaf tin with greaseproof paper. Spoon the mixture into the tin, smoothing the top.

4 Transfer tin to a roasting tin. Add boiling water to come halfway up the loaf tin. Bake for 1½ hours, topping up the water if necessary.

5 Remove tin from oven; cool for 30 minutes. Place a heavy weight on top of terrine (a second tin filled with cans). Place in refrigerator. Remove weight after 4 hours. Chill for at least 8 hours before serving.

Serves 8-12

Sesame Twists

1 x 215g (7oz) packet frozen puff pastry, thawed

60g (2oz) butter, melted

2 tblspn poppy seeds

2 tblspn sesame seeds

2 tblspn grated Parmesan cheese

1 Preheat oven to 200°C (400°F/ Gas 6). On a lightly floured surface, roll out pastry thinly to a rectangle measuring 30 x 20cm (12 x 8in). Brush with melted butter.

2 Combine poppy seeds, sesame seeds and Parmesan. Sprinkle mixture evenly over the pastry; press it down firmly, using a rolling pin.

3 Using a sharp knife, cut pastry in half to make two 30 x 10cm (12 x 4in) rectangles. Cut widthwise into 2cm (¾in) strips. Twist strips lightly.

4 Place twists on lightly greased baking sheets and bake for 8 minutes or until puffed and golden.

Makes 48

Continental Salad Sticks

4 cucumbers, sliced

1 green pepper, cut into squares

250g (8oz) cherry tomatoes

24 pitted black olives

Dressing

5 tblspn olive oil

2 tblspn lemon juice

1 tblspn chopped fresh basil

1 Combine the vegetables in a bowl. Mix all the ingredients for the dressing in a screwtop jar. Close the jar tightly, shake well, pour over the vegetables and leave to stand for at least 1 hour.

2 Thread the vegetables onto cocktail sticks or short wooden skewers.

Makes 24

Continental Salad Sticks

Chicken Drumsticks in Peanut Sauce

Chicken Drumsticks in Peanut Sauce

2 tblspn peanut oil

1kg (2lb) chicken drumsticks

2 onions, chopped

2 cloves garlic, crushed

1 tspn curry powder

1 tspn ground cumin

1/2 tspn grated nutmeg

1/2 tspn cayenne pepper

500ml (16fl oz) chicken stock

185g (6oz) peanuts, finely ground

1 Heat the oil in a large frying pan. Add the chicken drumsticks and fry on all sides until brown. Using a slotted spoon, transfer to a dish and set aside.

2 Add the onions and garlic to the oil remaining in the pan. Cook over gentle heat for about 5 minutes or until the onions are tender. Stir in the curry powder, cumin, nutmeg and cayenne; cook for 1 minute more.

3 Add the chicken stock and peanuts, bring to the boil, then simmer for 3 minutes.

4 Return the chicken drumsticks to the frying pan. Simmer, covered, until the chicken is tender. Drain and serve as illustrated, with cucumber sticks, sliced bananas dusted with coconut, chutney and red pepper diamonds. Supply cocktail sticks for spearing the vegetables and fruit.

Serves 10-12

Hot Rosemary Potatoes

500g (1lb) baby new potatoes, cooked

salt

60ml (2fl oz) olive oil

1 tblspn vinegar or lemon juice

2 tblspn fresh rosemary leaves

1 clove garlic, crushed

freshly ground black pepper

1 Cut potatoes in half and place in a baking dish.

2 Combine oil, vinegar or lemon juice, rosemary, garlic and pepper in a screwtop jar and shake well. Pour over warm potatoes and stand for at least 1 hour.

3 Preheat oven to 180°C (350°F/ Gas 4). Bake potatoes for 20 minutes or until heated.

Serves 8

Spanish Onion Frittata

3 tblspn olive oil

1/2 large Spanish onion, thinly sliced

4 eggs

salt and freshly ground black pepper

60g (2oz) mozzarella, coarsely grated

1 tblspn chopped fresh basil

1 Heat 1 tablespoon of oil in a frying pan with a heatproof handle. Add onion and fry over very low heat for 15 minutes or until soft and golden. Season. Transfer onion to a bowl; set aside.

2 Beat eggs. Season, then stir in cooled onion with mozzarella and basil.

3 Preheat grill. Heat remaining olive oil in clean frying pan. Add egg mixture, tilting pan to distribute evenly. Cook over moderate heat, without stirring, for 7 minutes, until bottom is golden and mixture is still runny on top.

4 Place pan under grill and cook until top is golden. Slide frittata onto a serving plate.

Makes 8 thin wedges

Fettucine Frittata

6 eggs, lightly beaten

250ml (8fl oz) milk

250ml (8fl oz) single cream

2 tblspn chopped parsley

1 red pepper, chopped

200g (6½oz) fettucine

salt

1 Preheat oven to 180°C (350°F/ Gas 4). Whisk the eggs with the milk and cream in a bowl. Stir in the parsley and red pepper.

2 Cook the fettucine in boiling salted water until tender or *al dente;* drain.

3 Stir the fettucine into the egg mixture and pour into a greased 23cm (9in) flan dish. Bake for 25-30 minutes.

Makes 8 thin wedges

Lamb and Spinach Mustard Strudel

3 tblspn oil

1 large onion, very finely chopped

350g (11oz) lean lamb, trimmed, very finely diced

185g (6oz) mushrooms, finely chopped

2 tblspn Dijon mustard

200g (6½oz) frozen chopped spinach, thawed, drained and squeezed dry

1 red pepper, finely chopped

2 tblspn chopped fresh parsley

30g (1oz) fresh breadcrumbs

6 sheets filo pastry

1 tblspn sesame seeds

1 Preheat oven to 180°C (350°F/ Gas 4). Heat 2 tablespoons of the oil in a frying pan. Add the onion and lamb; sear the meat quickly. Stir in the mushrooms and cook for 2 minutes, then transfer the mixture to a large bowl. Add the mustard, spinach, pepper, parsley and breadcrumbs; mix thoroughly.

2 Brush a sheet of filo with a little of the remaining oil. Top with a second sheet of filo, brush with oil. Repeat with remaining filo sheets. Spoon the filling along the short side of the pastry, 3.5cm (1¼in) from the edge. Roll up the filling in the filo to a firm sausage, tucking in the edges.

3 Place seam side on a baking sheet. Brush with remaining oil, sprinkle with sesame seeds and bake for 40 minutes or until pastry is golden. Slice to serve.

Makes 8-10 slices

Lamb and Spinach Mustard Strudel

Bacon Wrapped Prawns

125ml (4fl oz) olive oil

2 tblspn white wine vinegar

2 cloves garlic, crushed

2 tblspn chopped fresh oregano

24 uncooked king prawns, peeled and deveined, tails intact

8 rashers rindless streaky bacon

1 Combine oil, vinegar, garlic and oregano in a bowl. Whisk lightly, add the prawns and stir to coat. Cover and refrigerate for at least 1 hour, preferably overnight. Drain.

2 Preheat grill. Cut each bacon rasher into 3. Wrap a piece of bacon around each prawn, holding it in place with a cocktail stick.

3 Grill the bacon wrapped prawns for about 5 minutes, turning occasionally, until the bacon is crisp and the prawns cooked.

Makes 24

Seafood Brochettes with Dill Butter Sauce

16 scallops, deveined

16 uncooked king prawns, peeled and deveined, tails intact

8 cherry tomatoes

8 button mushrooms

1 green pepper, cut into 8 x 2cm (³/4in) squares

155g (5oz) butter

juice of 1 lemon

60ml (2fl oz) dry white wine

2 tblspn chopped fresh dill

1 Soak 8 wooden skewers in water for 1 hour. Preheat grill. Alternate 2 scallops and 2 prawns with 1 tomato, 1 mushroom and 1 pepper square on each skewer.

2 Melt butter in a saucepan. Add lemon juice and wine and simmer until reduced by one third.

3 Meanwhile grill brochettes for about 1 minute on each side until seafood is cooked. Stir dill into sauce. Spoon over brochettes and serve.

Makes 8

Cherry Tomatoes Stuffed with Prawns

24 cherry tomatoes

salt

15g (¹/2oz) butter, melted

125g (4oz) peeled prawns, deveined and chopped

freshly ground black pepper

1 tblspn lemon juice

snipped chives

1 Slice the tops off the tomatoes, scoop out the pulp, sprinkle the shells lightly with salt and invert on paper towels to drain.

2 Melt the butter in a small saucepan, add the prawns with plenty of salt, pepper and lemon juice; toss until heated through.

3 Fill the tomatoes with the prawns. Serve hot or at room temperature. Garnish with chives.

Makes about 24

Mustard Coated Courgettes

500g (1lb) small courgettes, halved lengthwise

30g (1oz) butter, melted

1 tblspn wholegrain mustard

1 Preheat grill. Brush the courgettes on both sides with melted butter. Arrange, cut side down, in the heated grill pan. Grill for about 2 minutes.

2 Turn courgettes over, brush cut sides with mustard and grill until golden and tender.

Serves 10-12

Bacon Wrapped Prawns

COCKTAIL HOUR

Small sophisticated snacks are the order of the day when cocktails are being served. Call them morsels, titbits or nibbles, the idea is to offer tasty, beautifully presented treats that can be disposed of in a couple of bites.

Mini Pizzas

Dough

500g (1lb) plain flour

1 tspn salt

1 x 7g (1/4oz) sachet easy blend dried yeast

300ml (10fl oz) warm water

Toppings

Choose from: tomato purée, grated cheese, sliced olives, sliced tomatoes, smoked salmon, prawns or shrimps, pineapple chunks, anchovies, sliced pepperoni, salami or ham, chopped green pepper, sliced mushrooms, sliced artichoke hearts, oregano, basil

1 Sift the flour and salt into a bowl. Stir in the yeast and make a well in the centre. Add the hot water to the well. Mix to a dough, then knead on a lightly floured surface for 10 minutes. Place dough in an oiled bowl, cover and set aside until doubled in bulk.

2 Preheat oven to 190°C (375°F/ Gas 5). Knead the dough until smooth, then form into balls about 4cm (1½in) in diameter. Place on greased baking sheets and press out into circles about 7cm (2¾in) in diameter.

3 Spread each pizza base with tomato purée, then add chosen toppings. Sprinkle with cheese. Bake for 10 minutes or until crisp and golden brown. Serve at once.

Makes about 72

Kitchen Tip

If a smaller batch of mini pizzas is required, freeze the remaining dough for use on another occasion.

Tray Pizza

Bake the pizza in Swiss roll tins for ease of cutting and serving.

500g (1lb) pizza dough, see left

250g (8oz) rindless streaky bacon

250g (8oz) button mushrooms, sliced

30g (1oz) butter

1 tspn sugar

3 x 397g (13oz) cans chopped tomatoes, drained

2 x 50g (2oz) cans anchovy fillets, drained

60g (2oz) pitted black olives

315g (10oz) Cheddar cheese, grated

1 Make the dough as described left. While it is rising, grill the bacon until crisp, then crumble it and set it aside. Fry mushrooms in the butter until tender.

2 Preheat oven to 190°C (375°F/ Gas 5). Knead the dough until smooth, divide it in 4 and roll out each portion to fill a 28 x 19cm (11 x 7½in) Swiss roll tin. Sprinkle the dough lightly with the sugar.

3 Spread drained tomatoes over the dough. Top 2 tray pizzas with bacon and mushrooms; 2 with anchovies and olives. Sprinkle cheese over all the pizzas. Bake for 20 minutes. Serve in squares or fingers.

Makes 32-48

Mini Pizzas

Carpaccio

Anchovy Toasts

12 salt-packed anchovies

1 clove garlic, crushed

¹/₄ tspn vinegar

olive oil, see method

freshly ground black pepper

1 French bread stick, cut into 1cm (¹/₂in) slices

1 Put the anchovies in a bowl with cold water to cover. Stand until all salt has been removed. Drain; remove all flesh from anchovy bones.

2 Preheat oven to 180°C (350°F/ Gas 4). Combine anchovies, garlic and vinegar in a food processor. Purée until smooth. With machine running, add oil in a steady stream until mixture forms a smooth paste. Add pepper to taste.

3 Spread anchovy mixture on bread slices, arrange on a baking sheet and bake for 10 minutes until heated through.

Makes about 40

Prawn Toasts

500g (1lb) peeled cooked prawns, deveined

6 spring onions, chopped

2 tspn grated fresh root ginger

2 tspn light soy sauce

¹/₂ tspn sesame oil

2 egg whites

6 slices white bread, crusts removed

30g (1oz) fresh white breadcrumbs

oil for deep frying

1 Combine prawns, spring onions, ginger, soy sauce and sesame oil in a blender or food processor; process until prawns and onions are roughly chopped. Add egg whites and process until combined. Spread mixture on the bread slices.

2 Cut each slice into 3 strips. Dip prawn-coated side of each strip in breadcrumbs. Deep fry in hot oil until golden brown, drain on paper towels.

Makes 18

Carpaccio

As the meat used for this dish is not cooked, it is essential that it is bought from a reputable supplier.

500g (1lb) fillet of beef

2 French bread sticks

90g (3oz) butter, softened

2 tblspn grated Parmesan cheese

2 tspn grated lemon rind

5 tblspn tartare sauce

2 drained canned anchovy fillets, chopped

2 tblspn capers, chopped

fresh parsley sprigs to garnish

1 Ask your butcher to cut the beef into paper thin slices.

2 Preheat oven to 160°C (325°F/ Gas 3). Cut the bread into 1cm (¹/₂in) slices. Place in a single layer on a baking sheet and bake for 10 minutes or until the bread is crisp but not dry. Set aside to cool.

3 Mix the butter, cheese and lemon rind in a small bowl. Spread the bread thinly with the mixture.

4 Place a slice of beef fillet on each bread slice, top with a little tartare sauce, anchovy and capers. Garnish with parsley. Serve at once.

Makes about 60

Avocado Sushi

Nori, wasabi paste and pickled ginger are available from Oriental food shops.

440g (14oz) short grain rice
750ml (1¼pt) water
5 tblspn rice vinegar
75g (2½oz) sugar
1 tblspn salt
5 sheets nori
2 tspn wasabi paste
1 small cucumber, peeled, seeded and cut into thin strips
1 avocado, cut into thin strips
1 x 60g (2oz) packet sliced pickled ginger, cut into thin strips

1 Preheat oven to 180°C (350°F/ Gas 4). Combine the rice and water in a saucepan. Bring to the boil, lower the heat and simmer, uncovered, until the water is absorbed. Cover the pan and simmer for 5 minutes more.

2 Mix the vinegar, sugar and salt in a small bowl. Stir the mixture into the rice. Arrange the nori sheets in a single layer on baking sheets. Toast in the oven for 2 minutes or until crisp.

3 Cut a strip about 4cm (1½in) wide from the narrow end of one of the nori sheets. Place the larger piece of nori in the centre of a bamboo mat, with the narrow strip centred on top; this helps to strengthen the nori during rolling.

4 Spread about one fifth of the rice over the nori, leaving a 4cm (1½in) border at the end furthest away from you. Using wet fingers, make a hollow horizontally across the centre of the rice. Spread one-fifth of the wasabi paste along the hollow. Mix the cucumber, avocado and ginger together. Fill the hollow with one-fifth of the cucumber mixture.

5 Use the bamboo mat to help to roll the sushi, pressing firmly as you roll. Remove the mat. Using a sharp knife, slice the sushi. Repeat with the remaining nori and filling.

Makes about 20

Avocado Sushi

Artichoke Bread Savouries

1 x 425g (13½oz) can artichoke hearts, drained

12 slices white bread

oil for deep frying

60ml (2fl oz) mayonnaise

1 tblspn double cream

1 tblspn snipped chives

2 tblspn chopped pimiento

dill for garnish

1 Cut the artichokes in half. Set aside. Using a 4cm (1½in) cutter, cut bread slices into circles. Deep fry circles in hot oil until golden; drain on paper towels.

2 Mix mayonnaise, cream and chives in a small jug. Assemble savouries by placing an artichoke half on each bread circle. Drizzle with a little of the mayonnaise mixture; garnish with chopped pimiento and dill.

Makes 12

Crabmeat Rice Cakes

250g (8oz) crabmeat, flaked

1 tblspn finely snipped chives

2 tspn finely chopped fresh parsley

¼ tspn dried marjoram

¼ tspn Tabasco sauce, or to taste

3 tblspn mayonnaise

1 tspn dry mustard

½ tspn white wine vinegar

salt

freshly ground black pepper

12 rice cakes

1 Combine crabmeat, chives, parsley, marjoram, Tabasco, mayonnaise, mustard and vinegar in a bowl. Mix well. Season.

2 Preheat grill. Spread crabmeat mixture on rice cakes. Grill until hot and bubbly. Serve at once.

Makes 12

Artichoke Bread Savouries

Cheese Spirals

1 x 215g (7oz) packet frozen puff pastry, thawed

2 tspn hot English mustard

60g (2oz) Cheddar cheese, grated

butter for greasing

cayenne pepper

1 Preheat oven to 200°C (400°F/ Gas 6). On a lightly floured surface, roll out pastry thinly to a rectangle measuring 30 x 20cm (12 x 8in). Spread pastry with mustard. Sprinkle half the pastry lengthwise with cheese, then fold other half over. Press layers firmly together. Cut into twelve 10 x 2.5cm (4 x 1in) strips.

2 Twist strips, pressing down ends firmly to seal. Arrange on baking sheets, sprinkle with cayenne and bake for 10-15 minutes until puffed and golden brown.

Makes 12

Watercress Sandwiches

1 bunch watercress, leaves stripped from stems

125g (4oz) butter, softened

1 tblspn chopped fresh parsley

1 tblspn snipped chives

1 tspn Dijon mustard

dash of Tabasco sauce

1 tspn lemon juice

salt

freshly ground black pepper

48 slices sandwich bread, crusts removed

1 Blanch watercress leaves in boiling water. Drain and squeeze dry and then chop finely.

2 Combine butter, parsley, chives, mustard, Tabasco and lemon juice in a bowl, season. Mix well, cover and chill for 1 hour.

3 Spread half the bread slices with butter mixture, cover with watercress and top with remaining bread slices. Cut in half diagonally.

Makes 48

Cheesy Nibbles

125g (4oz) plain flour

1 tspn dry mustard

125g (4oz) butter

125g (4oz) grated Cheddar cheese

1 egg, beaten

sesame and poppy seeds

1 Preheat oven to 190°C (375°F/ Gas 5). Sift flour and mustard powder into a bowl. Rub in butter until mixture resembles fine breadcrumbs, add cheese and mix well to a firm dough.

2 Roll out the dough on a lightly floured surface to a thickness of about 5mm (¹/₄in). Using small cutters (aspic cutters are ideal), cut out shapes. Arrange on greased baking sheets, brush with egg and sprinkle with seeds.

3 Bake for 10 minutes or until golden. Cool on baking sheets. Serve at once or store in an airtight container for 1-2 days.

Makes about 20

Devils on Horseback

30 no-need-to-soak prunes, stoned

30 almonds

250g (8oz) thinly sliced rindless streaky bacon

1 Preheat oven to 200°C (400°F/ Gas 6). Place an almond in every prune. Cut the bacon into short lengths just long enough to wrap around prunes, overlapping slightly. Secure with cocktail sticks.

2 Arrange on baking sheets. Bake for 12 minutes.

Makes 30

Devilled Nuts

375g (12oz) mixed nuts

125g (4oz) pretzels

60g (2oz) butter

2 cloves garlic, crushed

2 tspn curry powder

2 tspn Worcestershire sauce

¹/₂ tspn chilli powder

1 Preheat oven to 180°C (350°F/ Gas 4). Combine nuts and pretzels in a baking dish.

2 Melt butter in a saucepan. Off the heat, add remaining ingredients. Pour into baking dish and stir to coat nut mixture. Bake for 10 minutes, stirring once or twice. Serve hot or cold.

Makes 500g (1lb)

Devilled Nuts

Dolmades

Dolmades

1 x 185g (6oz) packet vine leaves, drained

salt

30g (1oz) butter

1 onion, chopped

1 clove garlic, crushed

110g (3½oz) long grain rice, cooked

2 tspn grated lemon rind

60g (2oz) slivered almonds, toasted

1 egg, lightly beaten

1 Rinse the vine leaves under cold water; drain thoroughly.

2 Heat butter in a saucepan, add onion and garlic and sauté until tender. Add to rice; stir in lemon rind, almonds and egg.

3 Place 2 teaspoons of mixture on each vine leaf. Roll up firmly, tucking in edges. Place the rolls close together in a saucepan. Add water to cover. Simmer, covered, for 30 minutes. Drain. Serve chilled.

Makes about 24

Crispy Parmesan Artichoke Leaves

3 globe artichokes

60g (2oz) fresh white breadcrumbs

125g (4oz) grated Parmesan cheese

4 eggs, lightly beaten

250ml (8fl oz) olive oil

1 Remove and discard two layers of leaves from the outside of artichokes. Cook artichokes in boiling water for 30 minutes or until tender; cool.

2 Remove and reserve outer artichoke leaves. leave hearts intact. Cut hearts into quarters.

3 Combine breadcrumbs and cheese in a shallow bowl; pour beaten egg into a second bowl. Dip bottom half of each leaf and all the hearts in egg, then in breadcrumbs.

4 Heat oil in a frying pan and cook leaves and hearts in a single layer until golden and crisp. Drain on paper towels.

Serves 10

Cheese and Chive Croquettes

220g (7oz) flour

500g (1lb) mozzarella cheese, grated

2 eggs, lightly beaten

60g (2oz) chives, snipped

1 tspn cayenne pepper

salt

60g (2oz) cornflour

oil for deep frying

1 Put 125g (4oz) flour into a bowl. Add mozzarella cheese, eggs, chives and cayenne, with salt to taste. Mix; shape into 24 balls.

2 Combine remaining flour and cornflour in a shallow dish. Roll balls in mixture until evenly coated. Deep fry in hot oil until golden. Drain on paper towels .

Makes 24

Bitterballen

15g (1/2oz) butter

3 tblspn flour

150ml (5fl oz) milk

155g (5oz) cooked meat, finely chopped

3 tblspn chopped fresh parsley

salt

freshly ground black pepper

grated nutmeg

dried breadcrumbs, see method

1 egg, beaten with 2 tblspn water

oil for deep frying

mustard for serving

1 Melt butter in a saucepan, stir in flour and cook for 2 minutes. Gradually add milk, stirring constantly until mixture boils and thickens. Lower heat and simmer for 10 minutes. Stir in meat and parsley, with salt, pepper and nutmeg to taste. Spread mixture on a plate, cool and refrigerate until firm. Form mixture into walnut-sized balls.

2 Roll balls in breadcrumbs, dip in egg mixture and roll in breadcrumbs again. Deep fry in batches in hot oil until brown and crisp. Drain on paper towels. Serve hot, with mustard for dipping.

Makes about 16

Garlic Tomato Stuffed Mushrooms

24 cup mushrooms, stems removed

juice of 1/2 lemon

15g (1/2oz) butter

l tblspn finely chopped onion

1 clove garlic, crushed

1 x 397g (13oz) can chopped tomatoes with herbs, drained

salt

freshly ground black pepper

Garlic Butter

30g (1oz) butter, softened

1 clove garlic, crushed

1 small spring onion, finely chopped

2 tspn snipped chives

1 Make the garlic butter by mixing all the ingredients in a small bowl. Beat well; set aside.

2 Wipe the mushrooms with a damp cloth, sprinkle with lemon juice and stand upside down on paper towels to drain.

3 Melt the butter in a saucepan, add the onion and garlic and sauté until soft. Stir in the tomatoes. Cook over moderate heat for about 20 minutes or until most of the liquid has evaporated. Add salt and pepper to taste.

4 Preheat oven to 180°C (350°F/ Gas 4). Place mushrooms, cups uppermost, on a lightly greased ovenproof dish. Fill with the tomato mixture. Top each mushroom with a dab of garlic butter. Grill until heated through and starting to brown on top. Serve hot.

Makes 24

Cheese and Chive Croquettes

SWEET SOMETHINGS

Whatever the occasion – picnic, patio party or cocktails round the pool – there's always a place for a platter of sweet treats. Even guests who deny eating dessert will find it hard to resist the mouthwatering morsels in this chapter.

Fruit Tartlets

Make the most of the best fresh fruit in season to top these tasty tartlets.

Pastry

185g (6oz) plain flour

2 tblspn icing sugar

125g (4oz) butter

2 egg yolks

about 1 tspn water

Custard Cream

2 eggs

1 egg yolk

125g (4oz) sugar

1½ tblspn cornflour

185ml (6fl oz) milk

60ml (2fl oz) single cream

1 tblspn Grand Marnier

Topping

1 tspn powdered gelatine

5 tblspn water

155g (5oz) apricot jam

2 tspn Grand Marnier

12 strawberries, halved or sliced

125g (4oz) seedless grapes, halved

2 kiwifruit, sliced

1 x 425g (13½oz) can apricot halves, drained and sliced

2 peaches, sliced

1 Preheat oven to 190°C (375°F/ Gas 5). Make the pastry. Sift flour and icing sugar into a mixing bowl. Rub in butter until mixture resembles fine breadcrumbs. Add egg yolks with enough cold water to make the ingredients cling together. Knead the pastry on a lightly floured surface until smooth, then divide into 12 equal portions. Roll out each portion to fit a shallow patty tin or small fluted flan tin. Prick pastry all over with a fork. Bake for 10 minutes or until golden brown. Set aside to cool.

2 To make the custard cream, combine the eggs, egg yolk, sugar and cornflour in a bowl. Whisk until thick and pale. Heat milk and cream in a saucepan until just below boiling point. Lower heat and gradually whisk in egg mixture until custard cream thickens. Remove from heat and stir in Grand Marnier. Cover closely and set aside to cool.

3 Make the topping. Sprinkle gelatine over water in a cup. When spongy, melt over hot water. Heat apricot jam in a small saucepan; press through a sieve into a clean pan, stir in Grand Marnier and gelatine mixture and cool until beginning to thicken.

4 To assemble the tarts, fill each one with pastry cream, levelling the tops. Arrange the fruit in a decorative pattern over the custard, brush with apricot glaze and refrigerate until firm.

Makes 18

Kitchen Tip

Do not allow the custard to boil after adding the eggs, or it may curdle.

Fruit Tartlets

Miniature Cream Horns

1 x 215g (7oz) packet frozen puff pastry, thawed

250ml (8fl oz) double cream

2 tblspn icing sugar

2 tspn cocoa

1 tblspn coffee-flavoured liqueur

1 Preheat oven to 190°C (375°F/ Gas 5). Roll out pastry to a 25cm (10in) square. Cut pastry into 1cm (1/2in) strips. Lightly grease 4 pastry cones. Starting at tip, wrap a strip of pastry around each cone, overlapping pastry slightly. Bake on a greased baking sheet for 10 minutes or until golden. When cool, ease off cones. Repeat until all pastry strips have been used.

2 In a bowl, beat cream to soft peaks with icing sugar, cocoa and liqueur. Chill. Spoon into a piping bag fitted with a star nozzle. Fill cream horns and serve.

Makes 20

Chocolate Truffles

110g (3 1/2oz) cooking chocolate, chopped

30g (1oz) butter, softened

4 tblspn icing sugar

2 egg yolks

1/2 tspn vanilla essence

desiccated coconut, see method

1 Melt the chocolate in a bowl over hot water.

2 In a second bowl, cream butter and icing sugar together until light. Gradually add egg yolks, beating well after each addition. Stir in vanilla essence and gradually add melted chocolate, mixing well.

3 Set mixture aside until it cools and thickens. Form teaspoons of mixture into balls; roll in coconut.

Makes about 24

Toffee Coated Walnuts

250g (8oz) caster sugar

60ml (2fl oz) water

6 walnuts, halved

1 Combine the sugar and water in a small saucepan. Stir over low heat until the sugar dissolves, then increase the heat to moderate and bring to the boil. Do not stir. Reduce the heat and simmer, without stirring, for about 10 minutes or until the toffee turns golden. Remove from the heat.

2 Using 2 teaspoons, dip each walnut half in the toffee. Place on a sheet of foil for about 5 minutes, to harden.

Makes 12

Cream Cheese Strawberry Tartlets

1 x 215g (7oz) packet frozen shortcrust pastry, thawed

125g (4oz) cream cheese

185g (6oz) ricotta cheese

30g (1oz) caster sugar

2 tspn vanilla essence

250g (8 oz) strawberries, hulled and sliced

2 tblspn passionfruit pulp

1 Preheat oven to 190°C (375°F/ Gas 5). Roll out the pastry on a lightly floured surface and cut sixteen 5cm (2in) rounds. Pinch the pastry edges to decorate. Arrange on greased baking sheets and bake for 10 minutes or until golden. Cool on a wire rack.

2 Meanwhile, beat the cream cheese, ricotta, sugar and vanilla essence together until smooth.

3 Spread the top of each pastry round with cheese mixture and top with strawberry slices and passionfruit pulp.

Makes 16

Miniature Cream Horns

Mixed Berry and Brandy Cream Tarts

Baby Florentines

60g (2oz) sugar

30g (1oz) butter

1 1/4 tblspn clear honey

1 tblspn single cream

22g (3/4oz) slivered almonds

1 1/2 tblspn chopped glacé orange rind

125g (4oz) dark chocolate, chopped

1 Preheat the oven to 200°C (400°F/Gas 8). Combine sugar, butter, honey and cream in a saucepan. Bring to boil over moderate heat; boil for 5 minutes, stirring constantly. Add almonds and glacé orange rind. Set mixture aside to cool for 5 minutes.

2 Line baking sheets with nonstick baking parchment. Drop 1/2 teaspoonfuls of mixture, about 5cm (2in) apart, onto baking sheets. Bake for 5 minutes. Remove from oven and trim edges to a neat shape, if desired. Return to oven and bake for 4 minutes more, until wafers are golden and bubbly.

3 Remove the baking sheets from the oven and let the wafers cool on the sheets for 2 minutes. Using a spatula, transfer the wafers to wire racks to cool completely.

4 Put the chocolate in a heatproof bowl and melt over a saucepan of simmering water. Remove from the heat. Brush a thin layer of chocolate onto the underside of each wafer. When dry, brush with a second layer. Make zig zag patterns on the chocolate with a fork. Allow the chocolate to set, then arrange the florentines on a large serving platter; chill lightly before serving.

Makes about 40

Kitchen Tips

If the wafers become too hard to remove from the baking sheets, return them to the oven for 1 minute to soften slightly.
The florentines can be made in advance and stored for a few days in an airtight container in the refrigerator.

Mixed Berry and Brandy Cream Tarts

185ml (6fl oz) double cream

1 tblspn brandy

1 tblspn icing sugar

1 x 215g (7oz) packet frozen shortcrust pastry, thawed

125g (4oz) raspberries, hulled

125g (4oz) blackcurrants, trimmed

1 Beat cream with brandy and icing sugar to soft peaks; cover and chill until required.

2 Preheat oven to 190°C (375°F/ Gas 5). Roll out pastry on a lightly floured surface and cut out twelve 7.5cm (3in) rounds. Line individual flan tins or patty tins with pastry rounds and bake for 10 minutes until golden. Cool, then remove from tins.

3 Fill tarts just before serving by spooning about 2 tablespoons of the brandy cream into each. Top with berries.

Makes 12

Brandy Snaps

125g (4oz) butter

125g (4oz) caster sugar

125g (4oz) golden syrup

125g (4oz) flour

1 tspn ground ginger

2 tblspn lemon juice

Filling

250ml (8fl oz) double cream

3 tblspn brandy

3 tblspn icing sugar

¼ tspn ground cinnamon

1 Preheat oven to 180°C (350°F/ Gas 4). Combine butter, sugar and golden syrup in a medium saucepan. Stir over gentle heat until butter and syrup have melted. Off heat, stir in flour, ginger and lemon juice. Mix well.

2 Line 2 baking sheets with nonstick baking parchment. Making one batch at a time, drop teaspoonfuls of mixture, about 7.5cm (3in) apart, onto a baking sheet. Bake for about 5 minutes or until golden.

3 Remove the snaps from the oven. Leave for 1 minute, then, using a spatula, quickly lift each snap and roll around a greased wooden spoon handle to form a tube; leave until firm. Repeat with remaining mixture.

4 Make filling by beating all ingredients in a bowl until thick. Pipe mixture into each snap; serve at once.

Makes 18-20

Fresh Figs with Orange and Grand Marnier

12 slightly underripe green or purple figs, stalks removed

250ml (8fl oz) fresh orange juice

60ml (2fl oz) Grand Marnier

1 Cut figs into quarters and place in a medium bowl. Pour over the orange juice and Grand Marnier, cover and refrigerate overnight.

2 Transfer chilled figs and orange juice mixture to a glass serving dish. Offer cocktail sticks or teaspoons for serving.

Makes 48

Fresh Figs with Orange and Grand Marnier

Chocolate Strawberries

125g (4oz) white chocolate, broken into squares

60g (2oz) white vegetable fat

500g (1lb) strawberries

125g (4oz) dark chocolate, broken into squares

1 Melt white chocolate with half vegetable fat in a heatproof bowl over a saucepan of simmering water.

2 Dip each strawberry into chocolate to cover bottom two thirds. Allow excess chocolate to drain back into bowl. Place on a foil-lined tray and refrigerate until set.

3 Melt dark chocolate with remaining vegetable fat. Dip strawberries again, this time allowing chocolate to come two thirds of the way up white chocolate. Allow excess chocolate to drain off. Chill.

Makes about 25

Rum Balls

185g (6oz) plain chocolate cake crumbs

2 tblspn icing sugar

2 tblspn cocoa

410g (13oz) dark chocolate, melted

60ml (2fl oz) double cream

2 tblspn rum

crystallized violets to decorate

1 Combine cake crumbs, icing sugar and cocoa in a blender or food processor. Add chocolate, cream and rum. Process until smooth. Transfer to a large bowl, cover and chill until firm.

2 Mould mixture into balls. Melt remaining chocolate and dip balls into it. Set on a foil-lined tray.

3 While chocolate is still soft, place a small piece of crystallized violet on top of each rum ball. Chill until ready to serve.

Makes about 30

Rum Balls

Pecan Crispies

3 egg whites

pinch salt

1 tspn vanilla essence

185ml (6oz) caster sugar

250g (8oz) pecan nuts, chopped

1 Preheat oven to 180°C (350°F/ Gas 4). Beat the egg whites in a large greasefree bowl until soft peaks form.

2 Add salt, vanilla essence and sugar. Beat for 1 minute more, then fold in the chopped pecans.

3 Line baking sheets with nonstick baking parchment. Drop teaspoonfuls of the mixture onto the lined baking sheets, 5cm (2in) apart.

4 Bake crispies for 2-3 minutes, then turn off oven and leave biscuits to cool for at least 1 hour. Using a spatula, ease biscuits off baking sheets. Store in an airtight container.

Makes about 72

Choc-Almond Fudge Squares

185g (6oz) caster sugar

3 tblspn golden syrup

125g (4oz) butter

1 x 250g (8oz) can condensed milk

250g (8oz) Nice or other plain biscuits, chopped

100g (3½oz) almonds, chopped

200g (6½oz) dark chocolate, grated

1 Combine the sugar, golden syrup, butter and condensed milk in a medium saucepan. Stir over low heat until the sugar has dissolved, then bring to the boil without stirring. Reduce heat and simmer for 5 minutes.

2 Off the heat, add the chopped biscuits, almonds and dark chocolate to the mixture. Stir until the chocolate has melted.

Choc-Almond Fudge Squares, Tuilles

3 Pour the mixture into a greased 20cm (8in) square baking tin. Chill until set.

4 Cut fudge into 2.5cm (1in) squares. Arrange on a plate and refrigerate until ready to serve.

Makes 64

Tuilles

60g (2oz) butter

2 egg whites

60g (2oz) plain flour

100g (3½oz) caster sugar

1 tspn vanilla essence

75g (2½oz) flaked almonds

1 Combine the butter, egg whites, flour, sugar and vanilla essence in a blender or food processor. Process until smooth.

2 Preheat oven to 160°C (325°F/ Gas 3). Line 2-3 baking sheets with nonstick baking parchment. Spread the mixture in thin circles, about 6cm (2½in) wide, on the lined sheets, leaving at least 4cm (1½in) between each. Sprinkle with almonds.

3 Bake the biscuits for 5-7 minutes or until golden. Cool for 1 minute. Using a spatula, remove each biscuit in turn from the baking sheet and flip it over a lightly greased rolling pin to create a curved shape. Leave until cool, then remove. When cold, store in an airtight container.

Makes about 24

USEFUL INFORMATION

Length

Centimetres	Inches	Centimetres	Inches
0.5 (5mm)	$^1/_4$	18	7
1	$^1/_2$	20	8
2	$^3/_4$	23	9
2.5	1	25	10
4	$1^1/_2$	30	12
5	2	35	14
6	$2^1/_2$	40	16
7.5	3	45	18
10	4	50	20
15	6	NB: 1cm = 10 mm	

Metric/Imperial Conversion Chart
Mass (Weight)
(Approximate conversions for cookery purposes)

Metric	Imperial	Metric	Imperial
15g	$^1/_2$oz	315g	10oz
30g	1oz	350g	11oz
60g	2oz	375g	12oz ($^3/_4$lb)
90g	3oz	410g	13oz
125g	4oz ($^1/_4$lb)	440g	14oz
155g	5oz	470g	15oz
185g	6oz	500g (0.5kg)	16oz (1lb)
220g	7oz	750g	24oz ($1^1/_2$lb)
250g	8oz ($^1/_2$lb)	1000g (1kg)	32oz (2lb)
280g	9oz	1500 (1.5kg)	3lb

Metric Spoon Sizes

$^1/_4$ teaspoon	= 1.25ml
$^1/_2$ teaspoon	= 2.5ml
1 teaspoon	= 5ml
1 tablespoon	=15ml

Liquids

Metric	Imperial
30ml	1fl oz
60 ml	2fl oz
90ml	3fl oz
125ml	4fl oz
155ml	5fl oz ($^1/_4$pt)
185ml	6fl oz
250ml	8fl oz
500ml	16fl oz
600ml	20fl oz (1pt)
750ml	$1^1/_4$pt
1 litre	$1^3/_4$pt
1.2 litres	2pt
1.5 litres	$2^1/_2$pt
1.8 litres	3pt
2 litres	$3^1/_2$pt
2.5 litres	4pt

Index

Editorial Coordination: Merehurst Limited
Cookery Editor: Jenni Fleetwood
Editorial Assistant: Sheridan Packer
Production Manager: Sheridan Carter
Layout and Finished Art: Stephen Joseph
Cover Photography: David Gill
Cover Design: Maggie Aldred
Cover Home Economist: Annie Nichols
Cover Stylist: Hilary Guy

Published by J.B. Fairfax Press Pty Limited
80-82 McLachlan Avenue
Rushcutters Bay 2011
A.C.N. 003 738 430

Formatted by J.B. Fairfax Press Pty Limited
Printed by Toppan Printing Co, Singapore

JBFP 294 A/UK
Includes Index
ISBN 1 86343 116 0 (set)
ISBN 1 86343 133 0

Distribution and Sales Enquiries
Australia: J.B. Fairfax Press Pty Limited
Ph: (02) 361 6366 Fax: (02) 360 6262
United Kingdom: J.B. Fairfax Press Limited
Ph (0933) 402330 Fax (0933) 402234